THE TRUTH BEHIND THE TRINITY

Finding the Light of Christ Beyond the Physical World

Treval Manne

Very Good Book Publisher

VERY GOOD
Book Publisher

This work is dedicated to George.
May his memory be Eternal.

FOREWORD

I have, in many times, and multiple ways, undertaken to explain my perceptual understanding and its implication on theology. I believe some people are well suited to receive it, while others will need to hear it to free them from limited perspectives, which prevent them from accepting a worldview which transcends the material world.

It is my hope, that if you are already a Christian, then you will see and understand the connections that I am trying to make between perception and theological reality. If you are not versed in Christianity due to a hesitancy drawn from an evidence-based objection, it is my hope that this work will loosen your materialistic convictions.

A warning before we go further: This is not a book for new Christians. If you are early in your walk with Christ, stop reading books about the bible and read it for yourself before you hear another's interpretation. The bible is a collection of books which must be met on its own terms and taken for what it is before you can entertain ideas like the following safely. Milk for the baby and real food for the adult lest the child choke on a morsel they are

TREVAL MANNE

unable to chew.

MATHEMATICAL BACKGROUND

The mathematics are primarily intuitive, but it is important to define some of the terms. In the zeroth dimension, there is only a point. A point, as defined by Euclid in "Elements," is that which has no part. A line exists if a connection can be made which connects more than one point. The line is a point thick (remember, essentially nothing) but can be infinitely long. There is, however, only two directions on a line: forward and backward. Distance is the main attribute that is noticeable in one dimension. A line segment can be defined by picking a point of reference and defining a distance between the reference point and a secondary point.

The second dimension is easier to understand. There are an infinite number of lines on a plane. A line can be defined with a reference point and a direction. This is taught in the context of a cartesian plane by having an origin point defined by a pair of coordinates, 0,0. The direction can be defined by an angle, such as 0 degrees, all the way back to 360 degrees being the same direction.

The halfway degree, 180 degrees, is the opposite direction from 0. The direction of a simple line on a two dimensional plane can also be defined by an algebraic expression such as $y=mx+b$ where y and x are the coordinates along two perpendicular axes, m is the slope of the line, and b is the point on the y axis which corresponds to the point on the line where $x = 0$.

Shapes can be defined by position as well as length and width.

A line, which is one dimensional space, has infinite points, and a plane, which is two-dimensional space, has infinite lines. Likewise, a three-dimensional space has an infinite number of planes. This fact is made apparent when we use magnetic resonance imaging. Each image has a plane with a width and a length. The plane, also called a figure or image, contains shapes depending on the reactions of the machine with our bodies. The number of images chosen is based on our needs for medical necessity, technological constraints, and time constraints, but there are an infinite number of two-dimensional planes in your body.

Each of the dimensions I just discussed can also be applied to time. As time and space are intricately linked, our experience of them is simultaneous. I will expound on these ideas as we continue to think about reality. In this chapter, it is enough to say that time is not stagnant, nor is it unidirectional.

PERCEPTION
OF REALITY.

When we look at the world, we can perceive things in our immediate vicinity using our three-dimensional organs. This observation should alert us to the restrictions imposed on our perception. Our eyesight allows us to see through some things but not through others. We can only detect the light which is in the visible spectrum. If you think you can know or perceive everything, you have deluded yourself or possess senses that I have not experienced myself.

Using our perception, we can see two dimensions with our three-dimensional visual organs. Our eyes are set up to see a grid of rods and cones. These specialized cells in our retina allow us this limited two-dimensional perspective of three-dimensional space. Using our experience, physical feeling, and our deductions, we can conclude that physical objects have at least a three-dimensional nature. We can remember previous frames, but that is just it, they are frames, not the full state of things. I use the word "state" to refer to a zero-dimension of time with a three-dimensional realm. A "frame" is zero-dimension of time with a two-dimensional realm. Because we can only collect frames, we must consider states over multiple points in time. We can deduce past states, because we can remember past frames. Therefore, there is at least a one-dimensional timeline. These are the safe decisions and going past them causes the reader to make speculations, and to accept more about reality than is plainly before them.

WHAT WE COULD SEE IF OUR PERCEPTION WERE BETTER

Beings with four-dimensional bodies have eyes that are four-dimensional, and sight that allows them to see the entirety of a state at any point in time. They have the ability to remember not only points in time, but lines in time. They can see the entirety of a timeline with all the entirety of the states within that timeline. No MRI needed. Changes to the timeline allow four-dimensional beings to deduce that there is a time plane, or more than one timeline that they can experience. Time travel is a possibility for those who transcend the perceptual limits of a single chain of events. Imagine an author deciding which course of events to send their characters on. They can make changes to the entire timeline for those characters without the characters knowing that a change has occurred. They can make such changes until they have published a definitive course of events.

COMMUNICATION WITH THE HIGHER POWERS

I like to use a certain analogy when it comes to the concept of revelation or communication with God or angels. I will cover the instances when such beings manifest in physical form. However, such manifestation is not necessary to influence lower dimensions. When you paint a picture and put a character in it, you have full authority over that character. As in a comic strip, you can change what they are thinking by merely changing the text within a thought bubble. Likewise, a higher dimension being, having the desire to alter the natural flow of our three-dimensional brains, can nudge us toward a different path or thought process. While we use text, the higher dimensional being can write thoughts into the brains of the creatures they have designed. Choice, then, can feel completely natural even if it was the result of the urging of a higher being.

INTERDIMENSION AL INTERACTIONS

Before we try to extrapolate further. I would like to discuss the implications of a fourth-dimensional body passing through one of the three dimensional states. A fourth-dimensional being existing above our three-dimensional realm would be able to effect change within the timeline imperceptibly if they were to move something either in our past, our present, or our future. Us being able to only perceive one point of time would mean that such a change would not be so simple to notice. If the fourth-dimensional being is benevolent, then such a change would be welcome to whichever person pleases that fourth dimensional being. It is my belief, that fourth-dimensional beings are often encountered by people who are seeking to communicate with them on the spiritual realm. I might have lost a few readers with this assertion, but it seems unlikely to me that beings with interlocking arms, eyes, heads, and other body parts should exist on this plane in the way that ancient texts described them. For instance, one of the kinds of angels in Ezekiel in the Old Testament, is described as being able to move in each direction without turning and has multiple heads, wings, and wheels with eyes all about it. This sounds like the description of a limited mind trying to describe a higher being that exists in a higher dimension, and therefore can only present portions of itself to a lower perception body.

Read the following Scripture from Ezekiel Chapter one verses five through twenty-five with higher spatial and temporal dimensions in mind.

"And in the fire was what looked like four living creatures. In appearance their form was that of a man, but each of them had four faces and four wings. Their legs were straight; their feet were like those of a calf and gleamed like burnished bronze. Under their wings on their four sides they had the hands of a man. All four of them had faces and wings, and their wings touched one another. Each one went straight ahead; they did not turn as they moved. Their faces looked like this: Each of the four had the face of a man, and on the right side each had the face of a lion, and on the left the face of an ox; each also had the face of an eagle. Such were their faces. Their wings were spread out upward; each had two wings, one touching the wing of another creature on either side, and two wings covering its body. Each one went straight ahead. Wherever the spirit would go, they would go, without turning as they went. The appearance of the living creatures was like burning coals of fire or like torches. Fire moved back and forth among the creatures; it was bright, and lightning flashed out of it. The creatures sped back and forth like flashes of lightning. As I looked at the living creatures, I saw a wheel on the ground beside each creature with its four faces. This was the appearance and structure of the wheels: They sparkled like chrysolite, and all four looked alike. Each appeared to be made like a wheel intersecting a wheel. As they moved, they would go in any one of the four directions the creatures faced; the wheels did not turn about as the creatures went. Their rims were high and awesome, and all four rims were full of eyes all around. When the living creatures moved, the wheels beside them moved; and when the living creatures rose from the ground, the wheels also rose. Wherever the spirit would go, they would go, and the wheels would rise along with them, because the spirit of the living creatures was in the wheels. When the creatures moved, they also moved; when the creatures stood still, they also stood still; and when the creatures rose from the ground, the wheels rose along with them, because the spirit of the living creatures was in the wheels. Spread out above the heads of the living creatures was what looked like an expanse, sparkling like ice, and awesome. Under the expanse their wings were stretched out one toward the other, and each had two wings covering its body. When the creatures moved, I heard the sound of their wings, like the roar of rushing waters, like the voice of the Almighty, like the tumult of an army. When they stood still, they lowered their wings. Then there came a voice from above the expanse over their heads as they stood with lowered wings."

The instructive part of this passage is that Ezekiel describes not only their appearance, but also their movement and the way that the four move together. Experienced through a vision, Ezekiel would be unable to perceive the entirety of the being, rather, the projection, image, figure, etc. of the higher dimensional beings would be sufficient to communicate what was needed in the visitation. None of the beings turned as they moved.

If a human were to project a second dimensional image for a second dimensional being to examine, we would not have to turn our projection on the plane to move it around. Instead, we would manipulate our three-dimensional body to move in such a way that the projection would translate without needing to turn in the two-dimensional space. Likewise with the wheels, Ezekiel describes the motion and adds in the twenty first verse that "the spirit of the living creature was in the wheels."

The spirit of the living creature is analogous to the spirit of a human. The spirit of a human, as I will discuss, is the higher dimensional body that casts its image on the three-dimensional universe. The spirit of the living creatures is the same spirit as the wheels that move with it. The spirit for the living creature is higher in the spatial and temporal dimensions, so it can be two places at once in the mind of Ezekiel.

Notably, the creatures, having the four rimmed, interlocking wheels, also had many eyes. Consider that for an angel, an array of eyes is similar to an array of rods or cones. The creatures, being able to sense all directions simultaneously while being projected into the vision world of Ezekiel is a manifestation of their ability to see beyond the world they inhabit. If the wheels of eyes are just the shadow of the angel's observational power, the true form and understanding of the creature would be incomprehensible to the human.

Here is an excerpt of an angel from Isaiah Chapter six verse 2 as well. Read it with the understanding of higher spatial and temporal dimensions.

"Above him were seraphim, each with six wings: With two wings they covered their faces, with two they covered their feet, and with two they were flying. "

My suspicion is that Isaiah, in seeing the multiple wings, was witnessing a blur of the shadow of the wings which were suspending the seraphim in the spiritual realm.

People throughout history have also claimed to be visited with the physical and tangible manifestations of higher beings. To explain how these beings interact in other ways, see the next chapter.

AN ILLUSTRATION OF INTERDIMENSIONAL INTERACTIONS.

If communication with four-dimensional beings is normal, and we can request their influence, their interventions are magical to us. An illustration might help. Imagine for a moment, that you have a sheet of paper. Assume the sheet of paper is a two-dimensional plane. Now, take a three-dimensional straw and pass it through the two-dimensional plane. To any observers living on that two-dimensional plane, a line magically appears where the straw passed through the paper. Upon examination, the observers conclude that this line has the nature of a circle. If they look at it from all sides, it will maintain its length. The shape will conform to the usual experience of seeing a circle. The cross section of a four-dimensional object would appear in an identifiable shape in this three-dimensional world in an analogous way. If a four-dimensional straw were to pass through our three-dimensional space, then a hollow sphere would manifest. Naturally, there are more complex objects than a straw or a four-dimensional straw, therefore I will not belabor the mechanism by which other four-dimensional objects might appear to us in the three-dimensional realm to our two-dimensional senses. Suffice it to say, that they would appear as solid as any other object. Indeed, many of the objects we encounter could have a fourth dimensional existence.

I hold that the higher dimensions than four-dimensional are harder to understand, yet extrapolations can yield thought provoking experiences. Imagine for a moment, that a being living in their four-dimensional body with their three-dimensional sight influences the will of a fifth-dimensional being. The four-dimensional being already can change which timeline is perceived by the choices that it makes. The choices of a five-dimensional being therefore, can change the complete set of choices, or in other words, change the rules of reality. The available states that the fourth-dimensional beings can access are only there so long as the five-dimensional beings observing the four-dimensional beings permit them to remain. If the five-dimensional being so wills it, they could move a four-dimensional being from one time plane to another. Such an action implies that there is a time cube made of a continuum of time planes. A five-dimensional being can deduce the time cube but cannot change the time cube they inhabit without the assistance of a six-dimensional being.

THE HIGHER
HEAVENS

Saint Paul writes in his second letter to the Corinthians in chapter twelve verses one through four about a man who claimed to have seen paradise in the third heaven.

"I must go on boasting. Although there is nothing to gain, I will go on to visions and revelations from the Lord. I know a man in Christ who fourteen years ago was caught up to the third heaven. Whether it was in the body or out of it I do not know, but God knows. And I know that this man —whether in the body or out of it I do not know, but God knows— was caught up to Paradise. The things he heard were too sacred for words, things that man is not permitted to tell."

When Paul speaks of things that are too sacred for words, I will not pretend to know what he means, because I did not experience what the man in the scriptures experienced. I suspect that, if there is a paradise in a higher heaven, then it exists in a higher spatial and temporal dimension.

Whatever the man glimpsed, he decided it was too sacred to share with others. The truths behind the machinations of reality are not something that can be shared easily or lightly with others. It is for these reasons I have not included everything that I know about these topics in this work and why the warnings for Christians early in their journeys was stated in the beginning. Still, I will give you a glimpse of a glimpse in the following chapters.

IMPLICATIONS ON THE TRINITY

The fifth dimensional being, interacting with the four-dimensional realms, would likewise appear as fourth dimension objects. Using those four-dimensional objects, they could also reach down and appear in our three-dimensional worlds. This, to me is one of the ways that I wrestle with the concept of the Holy Trinity in Christianity. The use of a three leaf Clover, or water being in three states has been quoted to me as an explanation of how God can be three persons in one being. I always found these explanations to be lacking in depth and explanatory power. Therefore, it is my belief that whichever dimension is highest, that is where the highest God resides, and that is the father. I will not attempt to define which dimension is highest, I suspect the seventh dimension is sufficiently high to allow for all the powers that we have thus far conceived for God. I will not limit the father to being confined only to those dimensions, but I cannot understand the implications of moving higher than the seventh dimension. If God the father was to interact with the sixth dimension, reach down into the fifth dimension, reach down into the fourth dimension, and then reach down into the third dimension with us, then the Son would manifest and become Incarnate of the Virgin Mary as an interaction which fertilizes an egg within Mary. Thus, the ascension of Jesus into heaven to sit at the right hand of the father is not hypothetical. It is not metaphorical. It is the actual seventh dimensional hand of God reaching down through each level of complexity in reality and using his son, his image on earth, to save all of existence. An image to us is a two-dimensional representation of a three-dimensional object. An image of God is a three-dimensional representation of Jesus's four-dimensional being. The fourth-dimensional being an image of the fifth, and so on until the culmination of God's Highest Unity and True self. Paul writes in his letter to the Colossians, "The Son is the image of the invisible God, the firstborn over all creation." He also continues a few verses later, "For God was pleased to have all his fullness dwell in him." Jesus also speaks about this oneness with the Father in his prayer for the world. In John Chapter seventeen verse eleven, Jesus prays, "I will remain in the world no longer, but they are still in the world, and I am coming to you. Holy Father, protect them by the power of your name, the name you gave me, so that they may be one as we are one." And again, he prays for those who hear the message once he has left the world, "My prayer is not for them alone. I pray also for those who will believe in me through their message, that all of them may be one, Father, just as you are in me, and I am in you. May they also be in us so that the world may believe that you have sent me." Jesus as the three-dimensional image of God makes the concept of the Father, Son, and Holy spirit easier to comprehend and accept.

OTHER VISITATIONS IN THE BIBLE

In the previous chapters, I discussed visions that the prophets described to the people of their time concerning the angels they observed. There are physical manifestations of spirits in the world which were recorded as well. I would like to go over them here. Jesus is a special exception because he was birthed rather than manifested in his entirety. Some of the people that you have met may be angels or demons that have interacted with the physical realm.

God himself has appeared physically to many people. The first such appearance was to Adam and Eve in the Garden of Eden. If my idea about the four-dimensional nature of the garden of Eden is true, then this was a four-dimensional visitation. Genesis Chapter three verse eight says, "Then the man and his wife heard the sound of the Lord God as he was walking in the garden in the cool of the day, and they hid from the Lord God among the trees of the garden."

Still, once humanity left the garden, God continued to abide with them. Genesis is full of stories where God visited and interacted with humanity. God speaks with many people, such as Cain, and he physically comes down from heaven as in the case of the tower of Babel. He also is seen to touch people as when he has a wrestling match with Jacob. In Exodus, Moses is permitted to see a physical manifestation of the back of the head of God. God can manifest in many physical ways. Sometimes as smoke as when leading the Israelites through the wilderness, sometimes as a storm such as when he appears to Job.

Angels are also permitted to take on physical form. When the angels visit Lot just before the cities of Sodom and Gomorrah are destroyed, they appear as young men who are physically attractive to some of the citizens of Sodom and Gomorrah. Likewise, an attractive man was the appearance of the angel that visited Shadrach, Meshack, and Abednego in the furnace. Nebuchadnezzar says in Daniel chapter three verse twenty-Five, "Look! I see four men walking around in the fire, unbound and unharmed, and the fourth looks like a son of the gods."

Also in the Gospels, Angels appear to the people in dreams and in physical form. To Mary, Gabriel the Archangel appeared, and to the shepherds, a host of angels appeared. Joseph received a Dream concerning Jesus' naming. In the acts of the apostles, Peter was escorted out of prison by an angel. He describes it in the seventh through tenth verses of chapter twelve,

"Suddenly an angel of the Lord appeared and a light shone in the cell. He struck Peter on the side and woke him up. "Quick, get up!" he said, and the chains fell off Peter's wrists. Then the angel said to him, "Put on your clothes and sandals." And Peter did so. "Wrap your cloak around you and follow me," the angel told him. Peter followed him out of the prison, but he had no idea that what the angel was doing was really happening; he thought he was seeing a vision. They passed the first and second guards and came to the iron gate leading to the city. It opened for them by itself, and they went through it. When they had walked the length of one street, suddenly the angel left him."

The ability of four-dimensional bodies to enter and leave the three-dimensional realm at will is something that seems incomprehensible to those of us who are constrained to the physical world at all times, but Jesus makes it clear that there is more to us than the physical reality that we can perceive. He says in the Gospel of John chapter seventeen prayer, "I have given them your word and the world has hated them, for they are not of the world any more than I am of the world. My prayer is not that you take them out of the world but that you protect them from the evil one. They are not of the world, even as I am not of it." Jesus is not of the physical world just as those who accept his message are not of the world. For those of you who are predestined to accept the word, your destiny is not to perish, but to have eternal life.

THE HOLY SPIRIT'S MIRACULOUS FOURTH-DIMENSIONAL POWER

The miracles of Jesus and his Saints are therefore not miracles at all, but, rather, invocations of the power of the four-dimensional bodies which are able to interact in the spiritual realm to affect change in the physical realm. Take, for example, the miracle of walking on water. The ability to walk on water could rely on the ability to change the physical properties of the water or the body so that Jesus can fight the attraction of the mass of the Earth. Another option is that this miracle relies on the ability to be independent of the law of gravity that governs the physical world. Imagine Jesus is a toddler holding a picture up on the television. The cartoon playing on the screen is subject to the laws that the animators put in the world of the show. The drawing that the toddler inserted into view may fall if the toddler so wills it, but it may likewise remain suspended on the air if they want the drawing to remain there.

Peter experienced the miracle in part. Faith in Jesus gave him a four-dimensional crutch on which his spirit leaned. This firmness of his faith faltered as he began to believe more in the water and metaphorically dropped the picture in front of the television.

In the spiritual realm, which I equate to the four-dimensional realm, a physical altercation is possible, and is very real to the angels, demons, and four-dimensional bodies of those who perceive in a three-dimensional world. The four-dimensional body of a human being is what I can best equate to a spirit. Your four-dimensional body can be pushed around, guided, and lead to influence the way that things are going here in the physical realm. Our consciousness, which, at least for now, is bounded to the physical world, cannot directly see these battles which happened very frequently, but can see the effects on people in the world. My suspicion is that when we are kind to one another and live in the law of love, our time plane is changed. I mean that the consciousness that is currently constrained is moved to a new reality where we are less likely to encounter demonic forces, or where the holy spirit has removed some of their influence on us. By our own choices, we can ask to be moved to a different time plain which will allow for different choices to be made on the physical realm. You might have noticed that there are some physical acts which really have no bearing on a moral or ethical decision. However, the things that make our decisions ethical seem to have real effects on what is possible.

If you have never entered into a group of faithful who believe in and practice asking for and performing miracles, you might not have experienced the changing of reality to accommodate the accumulation of spiritual favor to heal someone or speak in a language you have not learned, but these things have happened in my experiences thus far, and I encourage you to seek them out and abide in them. Do not seek them for the sake of the power that they have to heal your three-dimensional body. Do so for the saving of your spirit in the fourth dimension and the desire to become one with the church, the Son, the Holy Spirit, and the Father.

DIMENSIONAL DECAY.

The garden of Eden seems to me to be a four-dimensional paradise where spiritual fruits were universally available. For some reason, the spiritual fruit of the knowledge of good and evil had the result of making us need to be descended into a lower dimension of existence. It would be as though I forced you to lose your ability to see in frames, and to only be able to perceive lines and points.

Extending the punishment further, if you are two-dimensional body or to have some need to be descended to a lower dimension, you would then only be able to perceive points. If I descended you any lower, you would be nothing, merely a point yourself. You would not perceive any other frame but the one that you were in. This descension into the lower dimensions seems to be a punishment mechanism which will result, in the end, of the death of one's consciousness. The fact that God allows us to have a chance at redemption while we are this low in the dimensions is a true mark of his grace. Humanity, over the course of God knows how many eons, has been deemed unfit to exist in the presence of God in his purest state. We are components of God which will be burned up like weeds if we cannot be reformed. This reformation must occur through our conscious and voluntary ascension toward God's perfect love.

The Separateness of Consciousness, Perception, and Existence.

I am not sure of the implications of the constraints of time on consciousness which transcends the bodies that exist in each type of realm. There are numerous actions within and without our power which can influence what our conscience can experience.

When a consciousness is constrained to perceive a single frame, there is not much which can redeem it. It is stuck in a state of inexperience. I doubt that a soul in this state can think at all. To some this is the desired outcome. They wish to never experience the light of God. They desire to cease to experience suffering, even if it means to cease to experience love. The Love of God provided an escape, because, when Jesus died on the cross, he not only left his consciousness in the three-dimensional realm, but he also descended into each frozen frame. Whatever frame of being each consciousness was stuck in, Jesus freed that consciousness. The consciousness will be judged in the end of days. If the spirit is the fourth-dimensional body, the soul is the consciousness which experiences the physical world and the other worlds to which they must go.

THE FINAL JUDGEMENT

I mentioned before that I thought that the reduction of someone's consciousness to a lower dimension would necessarily remove them from existence. Whereas the perception of reality is limited in the third and second dimensions, the perception ceases in the first dimension. There is nothing to perceive on a line with no time or change. In the second dimension you are stuck in a single point of time, perceiving only one frame forever. In the first dimension, you do not have a recognizable existence. Even a line of infinite length has no width or depth. I cannot conceive what it means to experience less than a point of time. Jesus has made the trip from the highest heaven to each of the dimensions.

I believe the first dimension is reserved for those who are due for a second death. For those who have decided to cease to be and perceive. The souls will not be removed from the second death, for they are cast away into an inconceivable mode of existence. Most closely, I would call it darkness. In Revelation, it is called the lake of fire. God has graciously given us a chance while our consciousnesses still exist to have us turn from our evil ways. God's plan for dimensions below the third is to destroy them. Believers shall gain bodies like the angels. Prayerfully we have learned our lesson and purged ourselves of the evils that plague us in this layer of reality.

THE EUCHARIST

If you are a Christian, you have likely participated in the sacrament of the Eucharist, also known as communion. It is a very key element in the worship life of a Christian.

When Jesus was with his disciples, he took the bread broke it and said take eat this is my body which is broken for you for the forgiveness of sins.

When Jesus lifted the cup, he said take drink of this each of you for this is my blood of the new covenant which is poured out for you as often as you drink of it do it in remembrance of me.

When priests in the Orthodox and Catholic faiths pray over the bread and the wine, they are asking that Jesus would turn the physical elements into his True Body and his True Blood. Some faiths take this meaning to be metaphorical. Other faiths believe it truly becomes Christ himself. Understanding Jesus oneness with the church on the spiritual realm can illuminate this mystery along with other similar mysteries. When Jesus says that he will be with any two believers who are gathered in his name, he can do so. In his ascended state, he can check on each consciousness which is bound to a timeline and make his presence in multiple places at the same point of our time.

ENTANGLEMENT

There is a subject in physics concerning the effects of a phenomenon called quantum entanglement. An oversimplification of the subject reveals that the actions taken on one particle can affect another particle that is entangled with it. The Physicists and Mathematicians have discovered good descriptions of the effect and mathematically quantify the effect.

If my explanation is true, an illustration like the straw idea is in order. Imagine that you have a string made of three strands. If you observe the cross section at the end of the string, you may find that there are three distinct objects on the plane. The truth of the matter is revealed to the three dimensional being who can see that there is one string with three strands, connected very clearly together. A two-dimensional scientist would be unable to deduce the truth of the matter, but they could see that if they twist one of the strands, the twisting of the other strands is also affected. Certainly, a marvel to behold! But quite mundane for a being with the right perception.

MULTIPLE WORLDS IN PHYSICS

There are a few main theories that currently hold weight in the scientific realm. I encourage you to research more on your own as well with more scholarly sources. Quantum Mechanics has multiple interpretations that provide probabilities for the collapse of waveforms in the calculations associated with quantum events. For the Many worlds interpretation, the waveform does not actually collapse, but rather, both observations for each outcome are true in a different world. Other interpretations are more deterministic. The theories have some predictive power, but they are incomplete in ways that seem impossible to overcome with what we know at the time of writing. Without being able to communicate between two or more of the many worlds, the theory becomes unfalsifiable. Perhaps there is a more reliable way of communicating with higher beings that would allow for us to prove the truth of the time plane and its implication on the concept of free will.

By incorporating the concept of the multiple worlds into the scheme of things, I find it plausible that there are infinite combinations of quantum states which exist. The observers moving through and experiencing these states are aware of only one state at a time. They can experience one timeline worth of states per each consciousness. The soul that you play out has come to the end of this book in the quantum states that you have experienced thus far. There are other timelines that you could have experienced. The all-encompassing reality can be difficult to hold in ones' mind. Do not try to think about it too hard. You were not designed in your current state to understand such things in their entirety. In fact, if you were intrigued enough to read this book and want to learn more, I urge you to do so without forgetting the onus to abide in humanity with love and humility. Do not use this knowledge to lord over another, but rather, be a servant to all. Your neighbor could really be yourself in a higher dimensional expression of your soul or your soul's soul.

THE ALTAR CALL

If the depravity of your existence and the suffering in this world has convinced you of the truth of the sinful nature which separates us from God's perfect love, please know that you can accept his grace and mercy. Jesus died that you may have eternal life. No matter what you have done, true repentance and belief in Jesus can save your soul from the darkness. If you believe that you would prefer darkness to the glimpse of light that you have been allowed to see here on earth, I urge you to seek out more light, and to spread more light into the lives of those around you. Live a life of love and obey the commands of Jesus Christ of Nazareth. "Love the Lord your God with all your heart, soul, mind, and strength, and love your neighbor as you love yourself."

CONCLUSION

Thank you for enjoying "The Truth behind the Trinity: Finding the Light of Christ Beyond the Physical World" If this book has convinced you to accept Jesus, be baptized, or you would like more information about the faith, please reach out to a local Christian congregation.